BOOK REPORT BIG TOP

WRITTEN BY CANDY CARLILE
ILLUSTRATED BY BEV ARMSTRONG

THE LEARNING WORKS

INTRODUCTION

The BOOK REPORT BIG TOP is packed with a wide variety of highly motivational activities designed to make book sharing a rewarding experience for students.

Activities are arranged in order of difficulty within each section to allow for a wide range of student ability. A list of materials needed and step-by-step directions for students are components of each activity. Book report ideas are ideal for use with individual students, in small groups, or during whole class sharing sessions.

The BOOK REPORT BIG TOP is divided into five sections:

Fill-in Reports are activities that require little teacher direction.

Pencil Reports are activities that encourage students to express their ideas in written form.

Talking Reports provide students with opportunities for oral sharing of ideas about books.

Hands-on Reports are ways of sharing books through art.

Special Reports are for books on specialized topics, such as sports, science, adventure, jokes and riddles, poetry and more.

The BOOK REPORT BIG TOP also features Pocket Awards, which may be presented to students upon successful completion of any of the book sharing activities. These awards may be worn in pockets or used as book markers.

CONTENTS

Name _____

THE STORY BIRD

Write about your book on the story bird.

Name of My Book

Author

Best Part of My Book

Name _____

PICK A WINNER

1. Tell about your book by filling in the ribbon.
2. Decorate the ribbon with crayons.
3. Cut out the ribbon and pin it to the bulletin board so that others will know what a good book you read.

BOOK AWARD

Title
_____
Author

_____
Kind of Book

_____
Main Character
_____

My Name
_____
_____

Name _____

HOOK A BOOK

Write the name of your book and the name of its author on the fish below.
Tell about the part that you liked best.

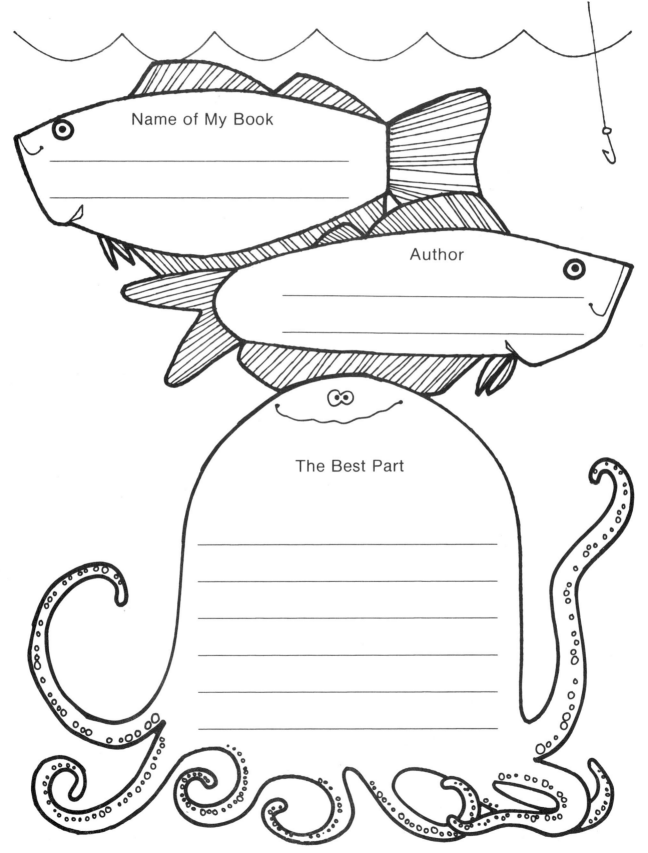

Name of My Book
_____
_____

Author
_____
_____

The Best Part
_____
_____
_____
_____
_____
_____

Name _____

BOOK BLAST-OFF

1. Write about your book on the rocket.
2. Draw a picture of the main character.
3. Color and cut out the rocket.

Name of My Book

_____

Author

_____

The Best Part

_____

_____

_____

_____

_____

_____

_____

_____

_____

Main Character

_____

My Name _____

Name _____

SPIN A TALE

What You Need

pencil	glue	
crayons or markers	paper plate	string
scissors	paper punch	

What You Do

1. Tell about your book by filling in the turtle.
2. Decorate it with crayons or markers.
3. Cut it out and glue it on a paper plate.
4. Punch a hole in the top of the plate and tie a string to it.
5. Hang your paper plate spinner in a place where friends can read about your story.

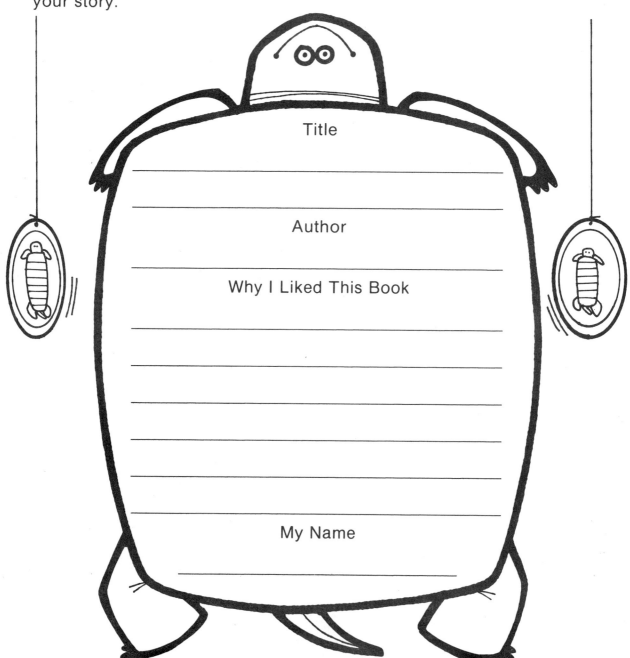

Title

Author

Why I Liked This Book

My Name

Name _____

COLOR A BOOK

1. Write a new word from your story on each crayon.
2. Write the title and author of the book on the box.
3. Color the picture.

Title of My Book

_____

_____

Author

_____

_____

Name _____

BOOK BALLOONS

Write about your book on each balloon.

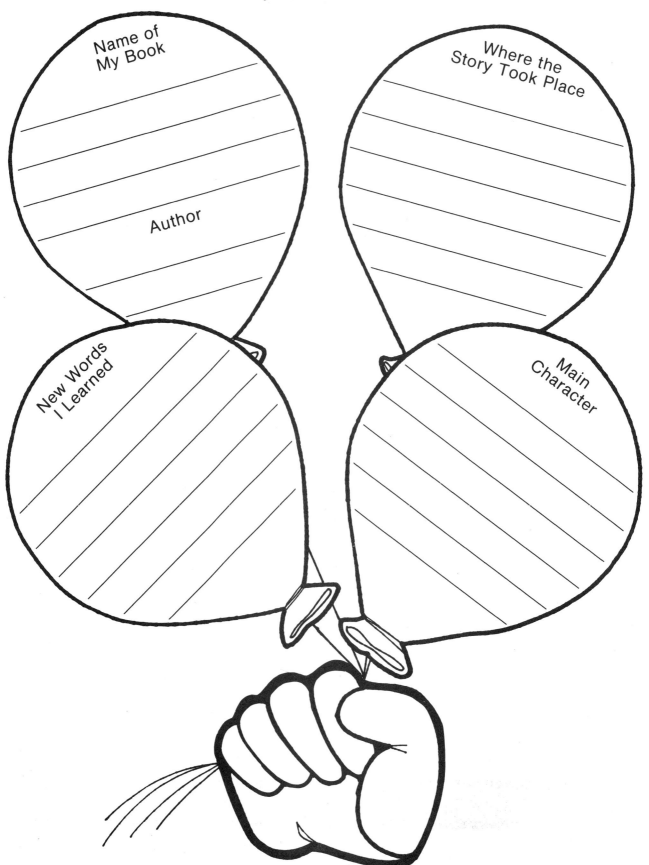

Name of
My Book

Where the
Story Took Place

Author

New Words
I Learned

Main
Character

Name _____

BOOKS-A-POPPING

Write about your book on the popcorn.

Name of
My Book

Kind of
Story

Author

Where the
Story Takes
Place

New
Words

Main
Character

Name _____

STORY SCOOPS

Write about three things that happened in your book.

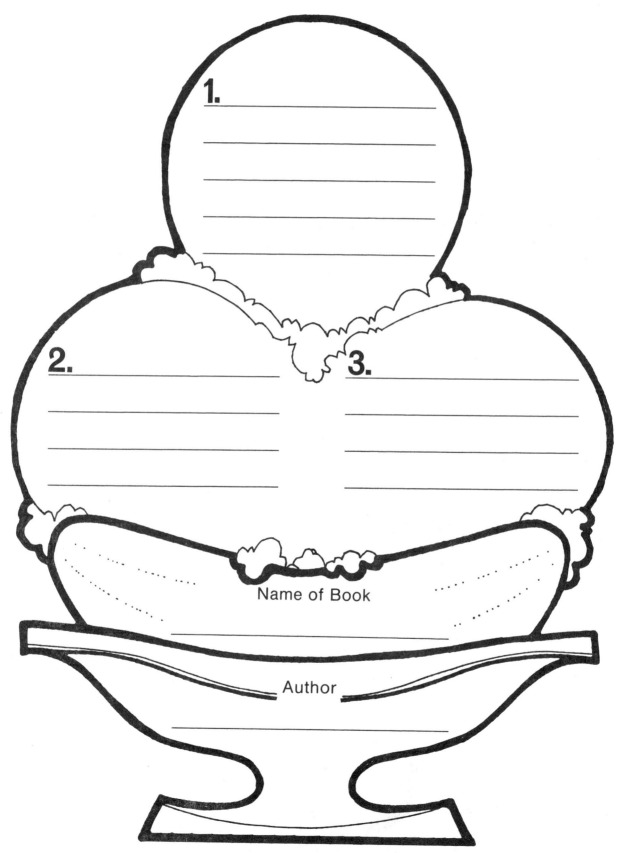

1. _____
_____
_____
_____
_____

2. _____
_____
_____
_____

3. _____
_____
_____

Name of Book

Author _____
_____

Name _____

LABEL A BOOK

What You Need

pencil   scissors

crayons or markers   tape or glue

empty soup can   ice cream sticks

What You Do

1. Tell about your book by writing sentences on the label.
2. Draw a picture to make it colorful.
3. Cut out the label and tape or glue it to the empty can.
4. Friends who read your book can print their names on ice cream sticks and put them inside your can.

Author

_____

_____

What was your book about?

_____

_____

_____

What was the best part?

_____

_____

_____

_____

_____

Title

_____

Name _____

SHARE A CARD

What You Need

      white paper (8½" x 11")
      crayons or markers

What You Do

1. Think of a special book that you would like to invite a friend to read.
2. Fold the white paper in half to make an invitation.
3. Write these things inside the card:
      Your friend's name
      The title and author of your book
      Why you think he will like it
4. Decorate the card with crayons or markers.
5. Give the invitation to your friend.

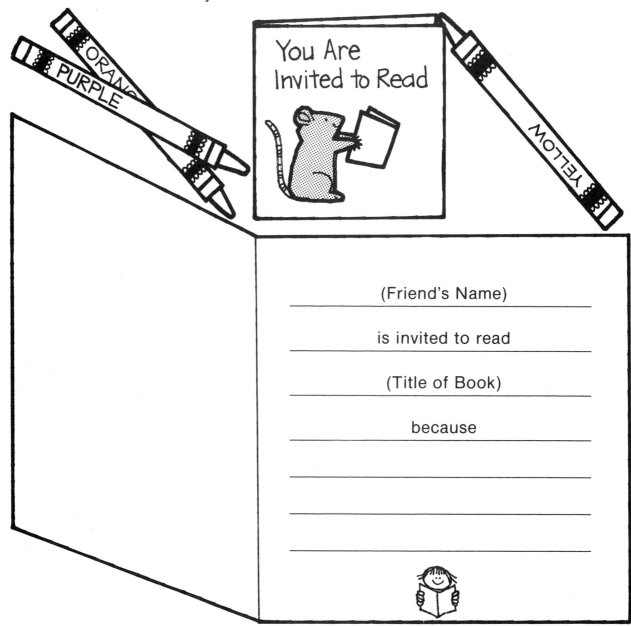

Name _____

FLIP A TITLE

What You Need
>   spiral index card (3" x 5")
>   crayons or markers

What You Do
1. Print the title and author of your book on the first index card.
2. Flip the title card up and print the first letter from the title of your book on the blank side of this card.
3. Write a sentence beginning with that letter on the lined card below.
4. Do the same for each letter in the title.
5. Be sure that your sentences tell something about the story.
6. Draw pictures for fun!

Name _____

STORY CUBE

What You Need

one shoe box without lid   crayons or markers
colored construction paper   glue
pencil   scissors

What You Do

1. Cover the box with colored construction paper.
   a. Cut a piece for the top, bottom, and each side.
   b. Glue the paper to your box.
2. Print the title and author of your book on the top.
3. On one side write a few sentences to tell about the best part of your book.
4. On another side draw a picture of your favorite character.
5. On the third side write five new words from the story.
6. On the fourth side draw a scene from the story.

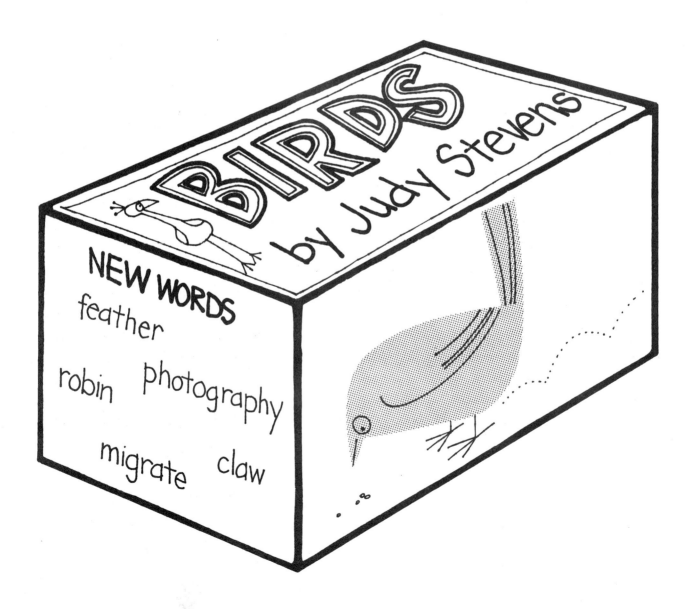

Name _____

A FOLDER FINISH

What You Need

manila folder

sheet of lined paper

3 envelopes

glue

crayons or markers

3 index cards

What You Do

1. Write the title and author of your book on the front of the folder.

2. Write a few sentences about the story on a sheet of lined paper.

3. Glue the paper inside the folder on the left.

4. Write the ending of the story on an index card.

5. Make up two other endings and write them on index cards.

6. Glue the envelopes inside the folder on the right.

7. Put one card in each envelope.

8. Have your friends read the story and try to pick the real ending.

Name _____

THE BOOK REVIEWER

1. Tell about your book by filling in the newspaper.
2. Write a sentence answering each question.
3. Draw pictures for fun!

BOOK REVIEWER

Title	Author
_____	_____

WHO? Tell about the main character.

_____
_____
_____
_____
_____   picture
_____
_____
_____

WHAT? Tell what happens in your book.

_____
_____
_____
_____
_____
_____
_____
_____
_____
_____

WHERE? Draw a picture of where the story takes place.

WHEN? Tell when the story takes place.

_____
_____
_____
_____

WHY? Tell why you liked the book.

_____
_____
_____
_____
_____

Name _____

STORY-VISION

1. Draw and color a scene from your story on the TV screen.
2. Write the name of the book at the bottom.
3. Show your story-vision and tell what you liked best about the book.

Name of My Book

_____

Name _____

PICK A POCKET

What You Need

pencil or pen   scissors
crayons or markers   straight or safety pins

What You Do

1. Write the title of your book and the name of the author on the pocket.
2. Add a few sentences telling why you liked the story.
3. Color the pocket.
4. Wear your pocket and tell your friends more about your book.

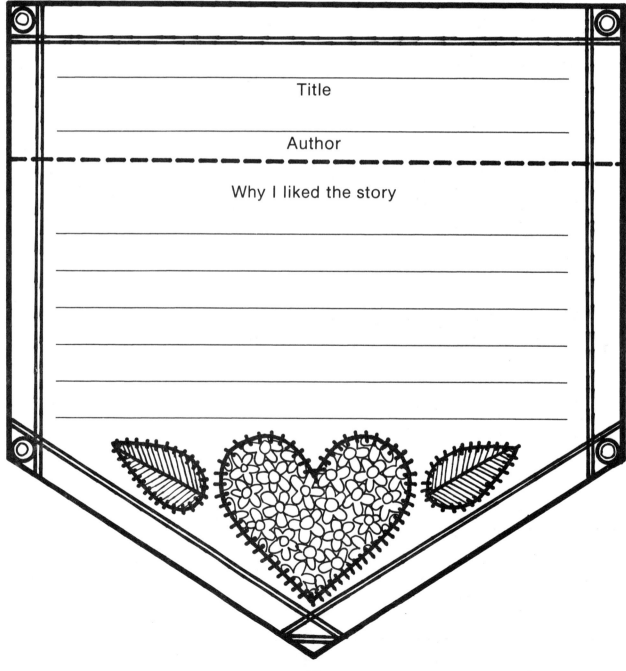

Title

Author

Why I liked the story

Name _____

STORY STRIP

1. Find a part in your book where the characters are talking.
2. Write their words in the bubbles on the story strip.
3. Draw the faces in the strip to look like the characters in your book.
4. Read your story to a friend.

Name _____

STORY WHEEL

What You Need

    crayons or markers
    scissors
    brad

What You Do

1. Draw and color four pictures from your book in the window squares on the bottom wheel.
2. Cut out both wheels.
3. Cut out the window square on the top wheel.
4. Put a brad in the center of the two wheels to fasten them together.
5. Tell about each picture as you turn your story wheel.

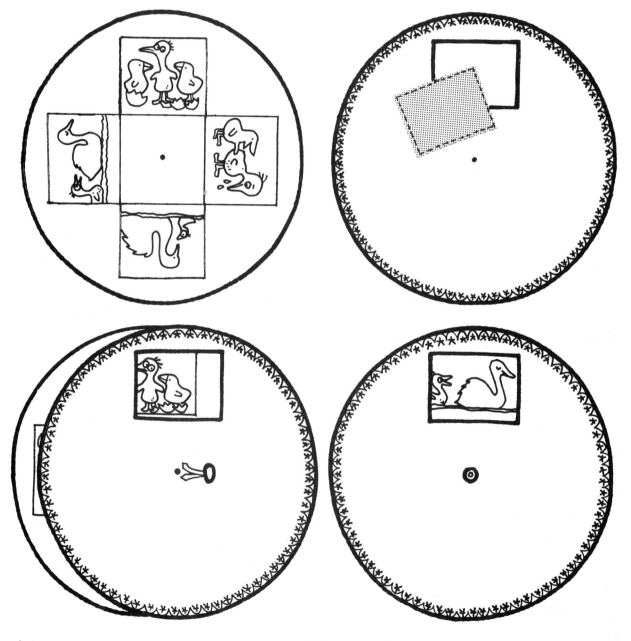

STORY WHEEL

Name _____

HIDE AWAY PUPPET

What You Need

paper cup   tape
scissors   1 straw
crayons

What You Do

1. Cut out the bottom of the paper cup.
2. Draw the face of a character from your book on the shape below.
3. Color the clothing.
4. Cut out the top of the puppet and tape it to the straw.
5. Use the puppet to help you tell a friend about the best part of your book.

Name _____

SHARE A ROLL

What You Need

2 sheets of lined writing paper
tape
pencil
crayons or markers

empty paper towel roll
two paper clips

What You Do

1. Tape two pieces of paper end to end.
2. Write things you'd like for a friend to know about your book on the paper. Leave about two inches at the top so you can tape your paper to the cardboard roll.
3. Add pictures.
4. Tape the top of your story sheet to the cardboard roll.
5. Roll up your story and hold it in place with a paper clip at each end.
6. Write the title on the outside.
7. Unroll the tale and read it to a friend.

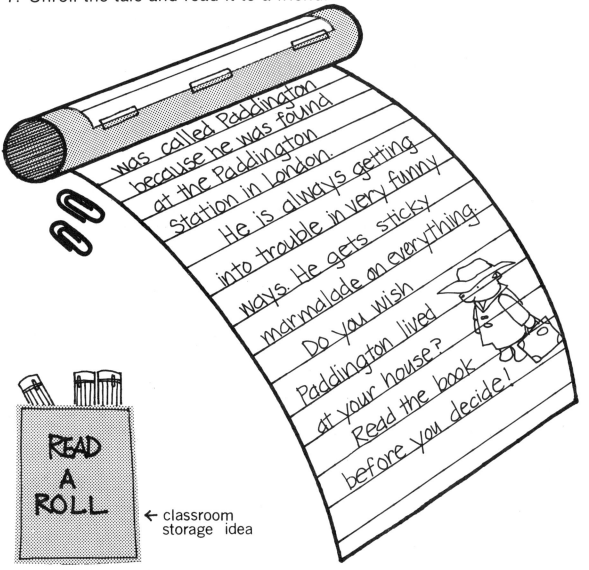

was called Paddington because he was found at the Paddington Station in London. He is always getting into trouble in very funny ways. He gets sticky marmalade on everything. Do you wish Paddington lived at your house? Read the book before you decide!

READ A ROLL

← classroom storage idea

Name _____

SANDWICH STORY

What You Need

2 pieces of poster board (12" x 24")
paper punch
yarn or string
crayons or markers

What You Do

1. Draw lines across each piece of poster board to divide it into three equal parts.
2. Punch two holes in the top of each board.
3. Using string or yarn, tie the pieces together so that they can be worn over your shoulders.
4. Print the title and author of your book in one square on the front board.
5. Write sentences about your favorite character and draw scenes from the story in the other squares on both boards.
6. Share your book by wearing the sandwich board and telling about each different part.

Name _____

TELL A TALE

What You Need

    large piece of butcher paper (3' x 4')
    crayons or markers
    scissors

What You Do

1. Pick one character from your book.
2. Draw and color a life-size picture of this character on your paper.
3. Cut out a hole for the head.
4. Stand behind the picture and tell these things about the character:

    Name _____

    Age _____

    Where I live in the story _____

    Who my friends are _____

5. Tell why this is a good story to read.

Name _____

T-SHIRT TALE

1. Design the T-shirt below to tell about your book.
2. Print the title of the book at the top.
3. Print the name of the author at the bottom.
4. Draw a picture in the middle.
5. Cut the shirt out and hang it on a clothesline in your classroom.

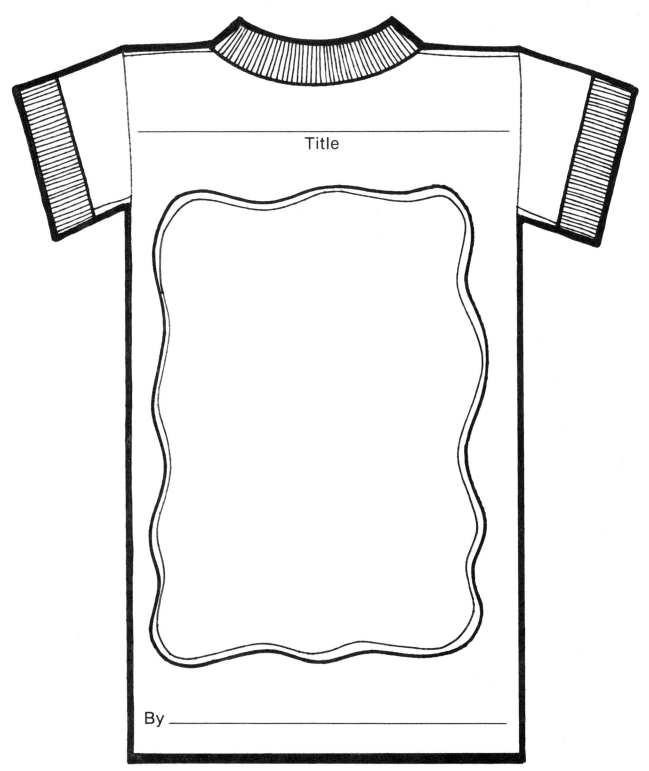

Title

By _____

Name _____

STORY SACK

What You Need

paper sack

crayons or markers

old newspapers

tape

What You Do

1. Print the title of your book and the name of the author on one side of the sack.
2. Decorate the other side of the sack to look like a character from your book.
3. Wad up sheets of newspaper and stuff them into the sack.
4. Tape the top of the sack closed.
5. See if your teacher can guess the name of your character.

Name _____

A FLYING DISK REPORT

What You Need

    2 paper plates   crayons or markers

    glue   scissors

What You Do

1. Glue the inside of the two plates together as shown.
2. Use crayons or markers to decorate the outside.
3. Tell about your book by filling in the circle below.
4. Cut out the circle and glue it on your flying disk.
5. When your teacher says it's okay, toss your disk to a friend.

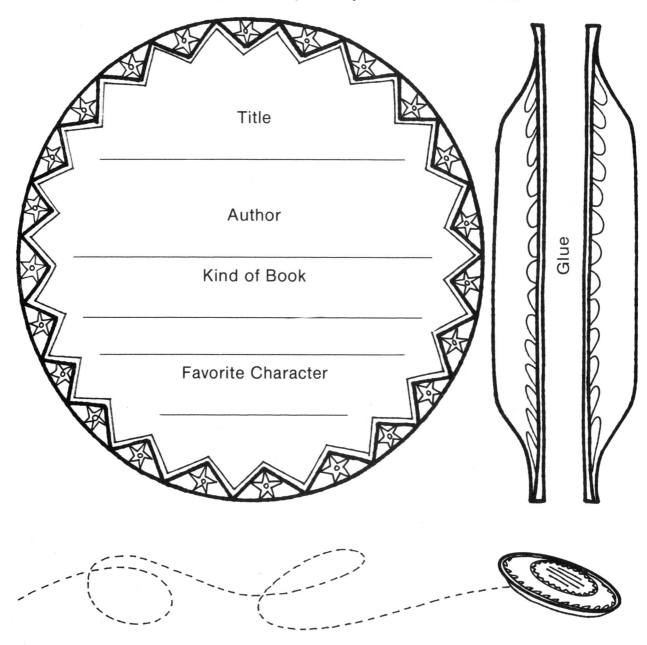

Title

Author

Kind of Book

Favorite Character

Glue

30

Name _____

PRETZEL PEOPLE

What You Need

paper plate
large bow-shaped pretzel
glue

crayons or markers
index card
tape

What You Do

1. Think about the main character in your book.
2. Glue the pretzel to the paper plate.
3. Draw the main character around the pretzel. Use the pretzel for any part of the picture.
4. Print the title of your book and the name of the main character on the index card.
5. Tape the card to the bottom of the plate.

Roger's Big Race
Roger Roth

Name _____

STRETCH A FACE

What You Need

clothes hanger

old stocking

yarn

construction paper

scissors

glue

crayons or markers

index card

What You Do

1. Decide on a book character you would like to make.
2. Bend the clothes hanger by pulling down on the bottom.
3. Pull the stocking up over the bottom of the hanger.
4. Tie it together with yarn at the top.
5. Cut and glue pieces of construction paper on the stocking to make the face of the character you have chosen.
6. Write the title of your book and the name of the author on the index card.
7. Glue the card on the back.

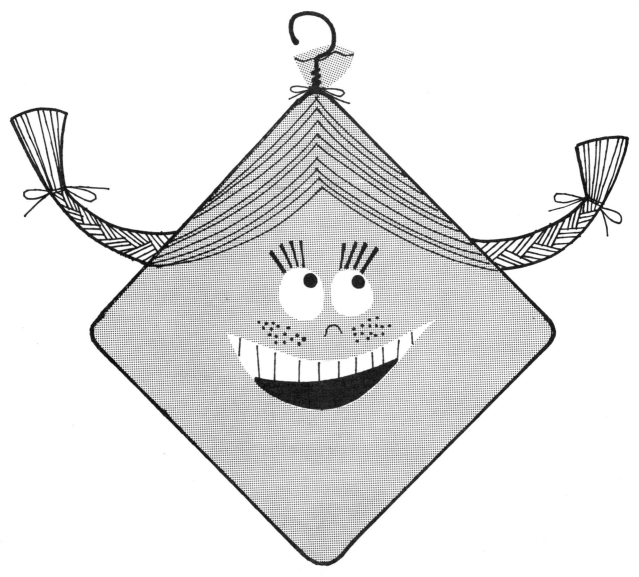

Name _____

PICK A STORY

What You Need

    light-colored construction paper
    crayons or markers
    box of toothpicks (flat on one side)
    glue

What You Do

1. Think of something from your story that you would like to make with tooth-picks.
2. Draw and color what you have chosen on the paper.
3. Glue the toothpicks on the parts that you want to stand out.
4. Let the glue dry completely.
5. Print the name of your book at the bottom.

A Bird in the Family

Name _____

PIN-UP PAL

What You Need

wooden clothespin   scissors
colored permanent markers   tape

What You Do

1. Decorate the clothespin with markers to make it look like a character from your book.
2. Cut out the paper strip and tape it to the back of the clothespin for arms.
3. Clip the character over the pages and one cover of your book to mark your favorite part in the story and share it with a friend.

Name _____

CAN A CHARACTER

What You Need

coffee can (1 lb.)   colored yarn
construction paper   markers
fabric scraps   paper strips (6½" x 2")

What You Do

1. Pick a favorite character from your book.
2. Make the coffee can look like your character by cutting out and gluing on pieces of construction paper, fabric and yarn.
3. Write sentences that tell about your character on strips of paper.
4. Put these strips in the coffee can.
5. Meet new book characters by sharing with friends.

Name _____

CHARACTER ALBUM

What You Need
> crayons or markers
> paper punch
> yarn

What You Do
1. Draw and color pictures of the characters in your book.
2. Print the names of the characters under the pictures.
3. Write the title of your book and the name of the author at the top.
4. Cut out this page and punch two holes where shown.
5. Use yarn to tie it with others to make a classroom album of storybook characters.

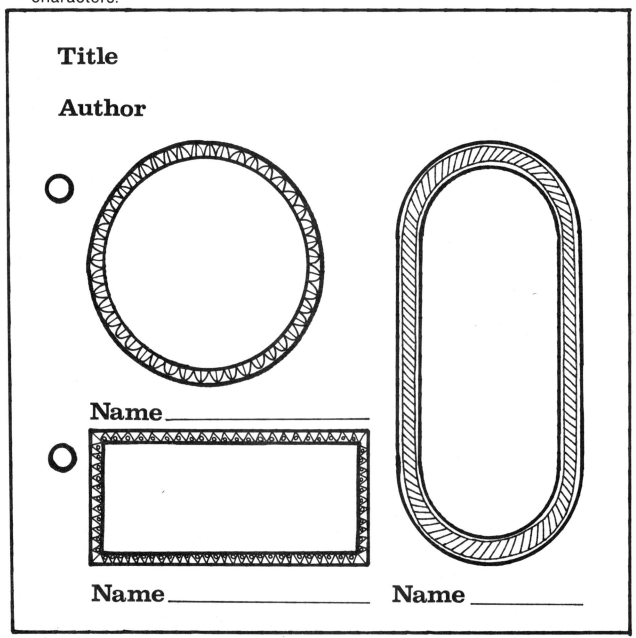

Name _____

READ A WINNER

1. Tell about your book by filling in the shoe.
2. Write the title of your book and the name of the author.
3. Write what sport the book is about.
4. Write two sentences telling what you learned about this sport.
5. Decorate the shoe.
6. Cut it out and show it to a friend.

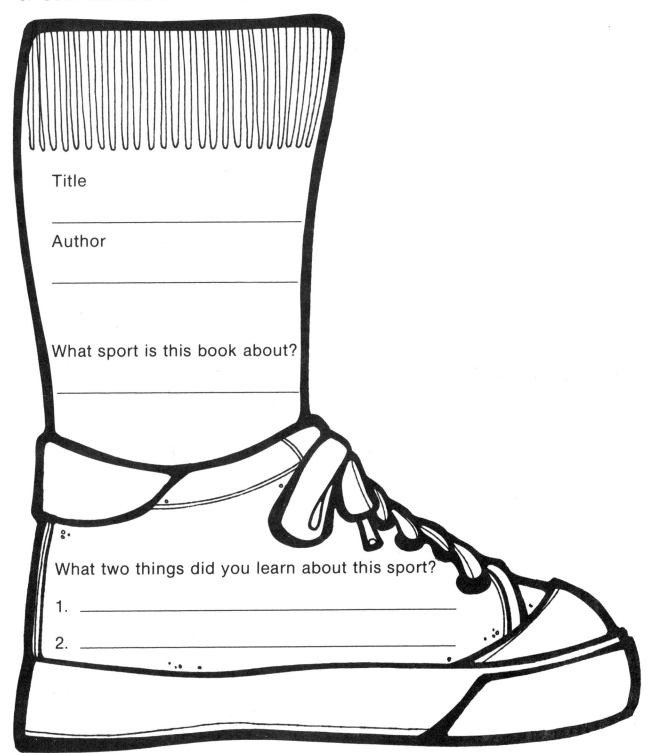

Title

_____

Author

_____

What sport is this book about?

_____

What two things did you learn about this sport?

1. _____

2. _____

37

Name _____

UP, UP, AND AWAY

1. Tell about your book by filling in the balloon.
2. Write the title of your book and the name of the author.
3. Write a few sentences to tell the most exciting thing that happened in your story.

Title

_____

The Most Exciting Part

Author

Name _____

WEAR A WORD

What You Need

colored paper strips (approximately 16) ½" x 6"
crayons or markers
glue or tape

What You Do

1. Write the title of your book on one strip. Write the name of the author on another strip.
2. Think of five new words from your book.
3. Write each of these words on a different paper strip.
4. Decorate the other strips by drawing pictures from your book.
5. Interlock the strips and glue or tape them together to make a necklace.
6. Wear your necklace to share your book.

Name _____

JAR A JOKE

What You Need

> large jar
> permanent colored markers
> tongue depressors

What You Do

1. Decorate the jar with colorful pictures.
2. Copy your favorite jokes and riddles on one side of the tongue depressors.
3. Write the answers to the riddles on the other side of the tongue depressors.
4. Add some jokes of your own.
5. Share your jar and a laugh with a friend.

Name _____

STORY PUZZLE

What You Need

   1 piece of white drawing paper (12" x 12")
   pencil
   crayons or markers
   glue
   1 piece of tag or poster board (12" x 12")
   scissors
   Ziploc plastic sandwich bag

What You Do

1. On the paper, draw a picture of the place where your story happens.
2. Glue the picture to the board.
3. Cut the picture into at least five puzzle pieces.
4. Put the pieces in the plastic bag.
5. Print the title of your book and the name of the author on the bag.
6. Share your puzzle with a friend.

Name _____

POETRY HANGER

What You Need

pencil or pen
lined paper
crayons or markers
glue

fabric scrap (9" x 12")
2 clothespins
clothes hanger

What You Do

1. Print the title of your favorite poem at the top of your paper.
2. Copy the poem on your paper.
3. Print the author's name at the end.
4. Add a picture.
5. Glue the poem on a piece of fabric.
6. Use the clothespins to clip the fabric to the hanger.
7. Hang your poem up in the classroom for others to enjoy.

Snakes

Snakes are funny.
They're long and slim.
It's hard to tell
A "her" from a "him!"

Candy
Carlile

Name _____

SHAPE BOOK

What You Need

pencil

2 pieces of heavy poster
board (9" x 12")

scissors

crayons or markers

white lined paper

paper punch

yarn

What You Do

1. Decide on a shape for your book report cover.
2. Using your pencil, draw the outline of this shape on one piece of poster board.
3. Cut out this shape.
4. Lay the shape on your other piece of poster board and trace around it. Then, cut the shape you have drawn so that you have a front cover and a back cover.
5. Use crayons or markers to decorate the covers.
6. Lay one cover on your white lined paper and trace around it. Cut out the shape you have drawn.
7. Write sentences on the paper to tell about your story.
8. Punch holes in your covers and paper, and tie your book together with yarn.
9. Write the title of your book and the name of the author on the front cover.

J.T.
by Jane Wagner

Name _____

STRETCH A LEG

1. Tell about your favorite tall tale by writing on this pair of jeans.
2. Write a few sentences telling about the funniest thing that happened in the story.
3. Cut out the jeans and use them to mark another funny part in your book.
4. Read this part to a friend.

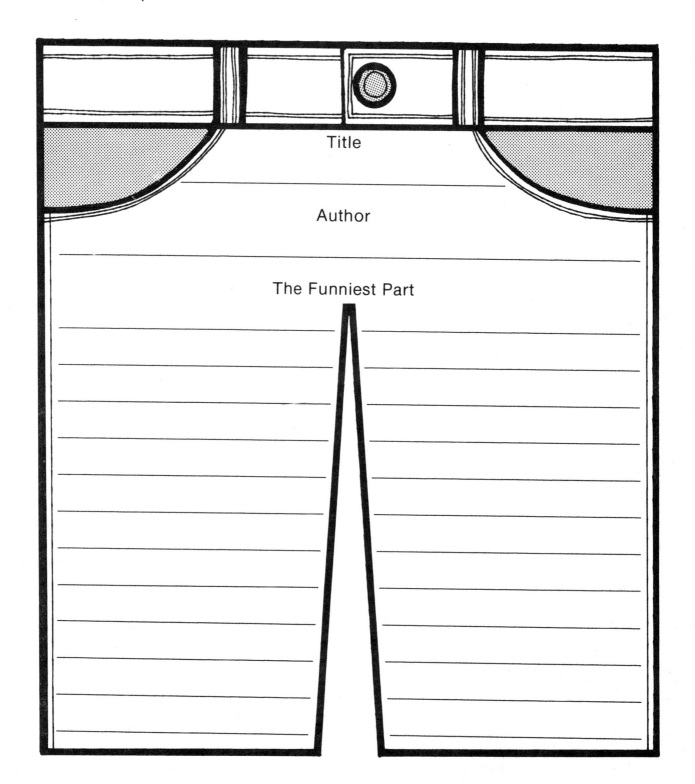

Title

Author

The Funniest Part

Name _____

MAKE BELIEVE MESSAGE

1. Pretend that you can send a letter to your favorite fairy tale character.
2. Write your letter on this page.
3. Decorate the page with pictures from your book.
4. Send the letter to your teacher.

Dear _____ ,

_____

_____

_____

_____

_____

_____

_____

_____

_____

Your friend,

_____

Dear Jack,
Trading the cow for those beans was a crazy idea!

Name _____

BOX A BEAST

What You Need

small milk carton   scissors
colored construction paper   index card
glue

What You Do

1. Think of a favorite animal character in your book.
2. Make the milk carton look like that animal by cutting and gluing on pieces of construction paper.
3. Write the name of the animal and the title of your book on the index card.
4. Put the beast with others to make a storybook zoo in your classroom.

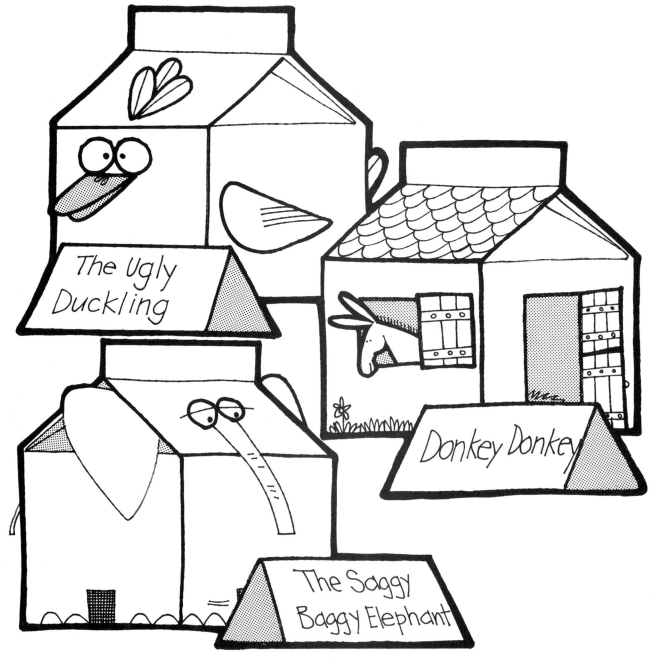

Name _____

CHARACTER FAN

1. Think of four interesting things about the main character in your book.
2. Write them on a piece of notebook paper.
3. Draw a picture of the person on the paper.
4. Make the paper colorful by decorating both sides.
5. Fold the paper into a fan shape.
6. Fan a friend and tell why you liked the character that you wrote about.

POCKET AWARDS

BEST BOOK REPORT

Name

_____

_____

FANCY BOOK REPORT

Name

_____

_____

MOST COLORFUL BOOK REPORT

_____

Name

SHARP BOOK REPORT

Name

_____

_____